Breccia

Breccia

MALCOLM CARSON

Shoestring Press

All rights reserved. No part of this work covered by the copyright
hereon may be reproduced or used in any form by any means –
graphic, electronic, or mechanical, including copying, recording, taping,
or information storage and retrieval systems – without written
permission of the publisher.

Typeset and Printed by Q3 Print Project Management Ltd,
Loughborough, Leics
(01509) 213456

Published by Shoestring Press
19 Devonshire Avenue, Beeston, Nottingham, NG9 1BS
Telephone: (0115) 925 1827
www.shoestringpress.co.uk

First published 2007
© Copyright: Malcolm Carson
ISBN-13: 978 1 904886 53 2

Shoestring Press gratefully acknowledges financial assistance from
Arts Council England

For Caroline

ACKNOWLEDGEMENTS

Acknowledgements are due to the editors of the following where versions of some of these poems have appeared – The Coffee House, Staple, Critical Survey, Orbis, Poetry Nottingham, Other Poetry.

Some of these poems have previously been published in *Take Five '03*, Shoestring Press, 2003.

An extract from *The Flood* appeared first in *Both Sides of Hadrian's Wall*, Selkirk Lapwing Press, 2006.

Mole in the kitchen won joint 2nd prize and *Clogher, perhaps* was Highly Commended in the Wolds Words Competition 2006.

CONTENTS

I	1
Clogher, perhaps	3
The Piano Teacher and her Pupil	4
We Have an Anchor	5
The Dung Hill	6
But then we were from different times	7
A Good Cut	8
Donaghadee	9
The Dreen	10
Belfast Lough	12
II	15
Edgar in Stanwix	17
Hadrian's Camp	19
On the border	20
Moving house	21
Carlisle-Newcastle	22
Edgar watches the heron	23
Dillon and me in Tarraby Lane	24
The Flood	25
Manna	28
Mole in the kitchen	29
Pariah	30
Tom	31
Cork & String	32
Edgar goes bait digging	33
III *Breccia*	35
Maiden Moor	37
Dale Head	38
Blencathra	39
Coledale	40
Black Combe	41
Skiddaw	43
Causey Pike	45
Helvellyn	46

Kidsty Pike   47
Carrock Fell   48
Caldbeck Fells   49

IV   51
Courbet in Sainte-Pélagie Prison   53
A Burial at Ornans   55
The Stone-breakers   57
The Catalogue   59
Pictures at an Exhibition   61
Drawings at an Exhibition   62
Fish   63

I

CLOGHER, PERHAPS

If I remember anything about that visit
it's the raid into the cabbages
twisting off the head
as you might from a mannequin
smelling the peppery freshness
as we stripped the layers
of thick veined skin to
the crumpled white cerebellum.
But then I also hear
my distant relative's
Do na', do na', I'll gie you a closh!
as we wanted another
his sense of waste prohibiting.
The ride on the pony
across the farmyard would not soften
the blow of his anger,
the fist of his accent
as certain and raw as cabbage stalks.

THE PIANO TEACHER AND HER PUPIL

'Do I hear the tide, Clive?'
as waves shuffled near her feet
deckchairs to the shore
where turnstones turned stones
among the wrack.
I looked to my uncle braced behind her:
her eyes, her aegis, glancing off
the mockery of family.
These were strangers to me
hidden behind the heavy brocade
of family's discretion,
their fugue only hinted at
across the years. She was
the predator, he the prize
polished for splendid hearths
in adequate avenues,
teacher and pupil, the left hand
for the right's dalliance
arpeggios of delight.
And then that leap
out of sight, the silent years.
My cousin once was thrashed
for meeting them for tea
above a cinema in town,
his impulse tawsed in turn.

WE HAVE AN ANCHOR

with acknowledgments to Priscilla Jane Owens, 1829-99

                                          Irregular.

I can see them still on the evening shore
As we played the games that they'd planned before
In their uniforms that they wore with pride
Just as sure in their faith as they were of the tide.

> *We have an anchor that keeps the soul*
> *Steadfast and sure while the billows roll;*
> *Fastened to the Rock which cannot move,*
> *Grounded firm and deep in our Saviour's love!*

I can hear them still in hymns that we sang
As the price that we paid and the sermon's harangue
About the depth of our sin and the only true Lord,
How our enemies would be put to the sword.

    We have &c.

I can see their wee feet as they pedalled away
On the organ they'd bring to Portballintrae
And the bellows would pump as the billows would roll
'Til the soldiers of Christ had won every soul.

    We have &c.

But our hearts were not there as our gaze would defer
To the rock pools and jetty, the dulse-laden air,
We would watch as the tide broke over the shore
And drew us away to life's great ocean roar.

    We have &c.

THE DUNG HILL

Each year it would be delivered
from Fletcher's farm at the end
of the cinder lane where I'd ride
my trike for days on end,
go newting in their pond.
Each year it would come in
a trailer backed up
to the garden gates where
I'd lost my mother's fork
by leaving it out, was
never forgiven as I've never
forgiven her for giving
my football programmes to
the Girls' Brigade Jumble Sale.
Each year we'd watch it
being teemed into
a hill beside the air-raid shelter
where John Spink, Peter McRae
and I would burn night-lights,
swear allegiance and death
and later Peter would die
on the airfield doing a ton.
Each year we'd tread it down
high on heady steam
up to our oxters in happy mire
spawning tales like mycelium.
And my father would say,
'It's for the roses,' but I know now
he was with us in the dung hill's
glory, dancing still despite himself
on his Cullybackey farm.

BUT THEN WE WERE FROM DIFFERENT TIMES

At our last parting I turned to your car, grim
with angry purpose for my train and saw
you hunched and obdurate as me, if not more so.
And in your look, our looks, there was a will

that would not soften to our blows before
time was called. Our wounds were open, raw,
beyond a suture from your surgeon's past,
blows to the heart, perhaps too hard to bear.

From that moment when I recall our rows
I fill with grief, flush with shame. But then
we were from different times.
                              As I pass
the photos of your wedding in my home
you're upright, proud, morning dress, patent
leather shoes, your bride, ready for life's dance.

A GOOD CUT

It was a tribal visit, when
my father would strop his accent

on gossip and crack,
talk of river flood,

of salmon flies and England.
As sheers nudged my ears again

and again, I saw the spinner in
the dark eddies of the Bush,

the catch-net in the reeds.
I recalled him at home

surgeon's hand subtle with
ligature for fly on hook

amid tins, reels and satchel.
Now we see each other mirrored,

me tented in gingham sheet,
him forward, elbows on knees

a flash of pride, content.
Then my long run across the beach.

DONAGHADEE

'A good Protestant sea, that,' said my cousin,
his face towards the Copelands
and the crack of early morning wind.
He dried the water from
his scaldy's neck to bloodless toes
with towel laundered barnacle-harsh.
An exile's son, still
I knew what he meant, could see
in the waves' swell and suck
the black flails of wrack
and thongweed that make
you kick out for the rocks
to clasp limpet-sure,
knees tucked to juddering chin;
could see the pools emptied of
the silliness of basking hours,
anemones now nipple hard.
And as I watched blood smudge
a delta from his chafed knee
I remembered the cacophony of families
– Strahans, Carsons, Craigs –
on ancestral picnics
in those Antrim coves,
and the English boy apart
in the rockpool's calm.

THE DREEN

Her eyes narrowed when I asked the way,
body turned like a question mark.
She told enough for me, for her
in case blame should later be attached.
We made our way out of the village
past my father's school, church,
Loyal Orange Lodge which he despised
– freemasons later drew him in –
up the narrow hill to where
The Dreen announced itself in shadow.
We'd pried too far for discretion
so turned into the drive
stopped like hawkers in front
expecting inherited proprieties
at best, Presbyterian decencies
as structured as the house.
This owner welcomed us
with almost open arms
took us through the door
I knew from the painting
to the foot of the stairs.
I ran my hand on the banister's grain
added to the patina, looked
to hear ancestral voices: father, his sisters
hushed to bedrooms with admonitions.
Through the kitchen, scullery
to a mossy yard beneath the beeches.
I would have handled the stable walls
where my father kept the pony
that drew his trap to school,
would've liked to admire the lichens
on those Irish pillars that gated
the broken walk through rhododendrons,
have taken in the whole, dank with memory.

Our host though had other plans.
He wished a show, terpsichorean in extravagance,

for out of his car boot — some anxiety there —
he drew his juggling clubs, his paraphernalia,
took on motley. His tricks lit
the Antrim sky as my sons watched
his dexterity, entranced.
His talk of travel, Papua New Guinea,
Pidgin English and tight-rope walks
coruscated beneath the beeches.
He told us of circus acts, showed us
the lake he was making, made dance
the diggers like giant caddis flies.
Then as we left he seemed to rise
like Chagall's lovers above
The Dreen's sound walls.

BELFAST LOUGH

Such a long time it had been.
Gannets and terns saw us in,
stabbing memories into life with
their considered dives where sea
gave up to darker waters of the docks,
wheeled away. Cranes, rigs,
containers, flats, mountains,
smell of oil, dulse and dialect.
I was inviting them in, sons and wife,
to my remembered past.
Taste this, know my separation
from friends: new school, new sport,
new name, or way of saying it
to stop the mimics. Blithely
I had sauntered through
The Markets, learned Louis and Miles
before that vicious time, the bus
back home beneath Stormont's basilisk
where once my dog pissed
on our namesake's plinth.

Now splendid roads up north past places
out of bulletins, then Ballymena,
Cullybackey, Ballymoney, Bushmills,
Portballintrae, the shore, my rock pool.
Limpets, anemones, shrimps and crabs
descendants of the ones I'd catch
unawares and often.
'Cowrie, cowrie, come to me,
Come to me from the deep blue sea,'
my mother would sing
as now we sing.
The *Claire Louise* high up the harbour
where my brother had dived
flat enough to miss the flagellant weed,
toes white at the edge of the wall.
Cushendall, Cushendun, a challenge to bathe

in that cold Whit week, goose flesh
like barnacles, bloodied knees.
High service at Maggy Scally's, breakfasts
as grand as a sideboard. We pitched up
on beaches as blown and brisk
as Moody and Sankey,
built giant causeways
that run across the years.

II

EDGAR IN STANWIX

Traffic lights on Stanwix Bank.
I sup the smell of resin from
bark of logs from Borders hills
stacked high and neat as matches
on juggernauts that strain and lurch
against their brakes in a fog of fumes.
In the Crown I settle to
others' banter, take comfort from
apartness, work on the riddle
of myself amid all this.
Poor Tom, look at stains
on chairs and faces through filter of smoke
grotesqueries of teeth, leers,
see reflected what I imagine is
myself in mirrors above the bar.
Too many of me here. Am I all
the same? Whose meagre crown is this,
on Scotland Road? Do I belong
north or south? I turn to the window
see the cyber café close,
logging off identities
across the ether that settle in
the mind, as real as blood, as ratsbane.
O! do de, do de, do de.
In Tarraby Lane I count the hedge:
holly, alder, maple, beech,
plashed, pleached, layered – where am
I from? Sheep avoid me as does
the pelting moon above the vallum.
Do I hear cavalry's drum on the plain?
Spectres who stripped others of
their souls – unhappy ditto – fashioned
new selves that sit as well as armour.
Should I look in this marsh pool, draw
aside its oily curtain, find

someone looking out beyond
my best, my worst imaginings?
I can pick kingdoms in the bark
of hawthorn, split them, make bigger
on a whim. I can sleep with the holly
against my cheek, suffer cold winds
and persecutions of the sky.
Why then, Tom…Edgar is all one?

HADRIAN'S CAMP

Fascias, rooflines, seamless gutters
such is the stuff that's peddled now
through suburbs where the pieris glows.

We never see who buys yet someone must.
Tinkers, potters, hawkers, 'A'y rag bone?'
were part of childhood before

those pulsing transits throbbed their way
to town or job, braggadocios
from the camp, just at the edge.

Yet still those fists that steer
will rein the pony through
Appleby streets, Eden's rocky bed

in a clatter of hoofs and heart,
clasp on bargain, spill out
the coinage of their inherited purse.

ON THE BORDER

A rap on the pane sends them up, corvidae –
jackdaw, crow and rook. Attendant starlings,
scullions in the pecking order, clear away.
Across the allotment to the ancient hedge

high above the sweep of the sleeping Wall
to the beech wood, they flock.
We are at the edge of suburb where
nature's reivers should be politer sorts.

But while we think our gardens firm estates,
emblems of order in a disordered spring,
they caper like drunken elders, glistening black,
deviscerate the shrew on tended lawn.

MOVING HOUSE

Like turning over in bed, really,
to the habitation of another dream
as inconclusive as the last.

Around the window-frame the dust
of sleep, the lichen from conversations
distilled against night glass.

Things are boxed from our different selves
– trainers with books, bills with clocks –
forming improper relationships.

The cat mooches within this lair of a house,
avoids another's scrat and scent,
shuffles its own contiguity.

In the shed for a while, the plants grow pale
etiolate like tentative friendships
across a distance now too far.

CARLISLE – NEWCASTLE

I wish I could tell what birds they were
that annotated the power lines,
watch that birch topple to the stagnant pool
with its weight of moss,
see the mine water clear
from Blenkinsopp pit
in its treatment bed like the lees
of a heady brew,
find out which sheep reached the end
of the field first as they were spun
like wet jumpers by
this careering drum of a train,
smell viburnum sweet
by the tiny platform that waits
for passengers, know how soon
mist will clear from the drills
of winter wheat, watch the crow settle
by the warren, that sedge dry to stiffness,
goosander rise out of the icy South Tyne,
know why that rabbit was black
and when the Range Rover was put up on bricks.

Giddy with it all I can only settle back
contrive landscapes of my own,
hope to know those.

EDGAR WATCHES THE HERON

I am done with the foul fiend
– Tom haunts the hawthorn
on the windy slope
like antique plastic
on by-pass fence.
                       I am here
above the river called Eden
running black as brother's deeds,
father's ignorance, my knowledge.
I watch the heron in the marbled eddies
that catch the moon.
His eye's the thing
which gives a meaning to the rest;
such fastidious engineering
a lethal reed that will wait,
wait for the lazy bask
of salmon, strike.
I need its patience, the breath
of earnest concentration,
need to know the moment
just as the moon torches through
the shattered cloud.

DILLON AND ME IN TARRABY LANE

We needed to move them, ash and maple,
taken too well in our ordered wilderness.
Spade, boots and bag with roots
that seemed to clench the mulch
of Tarraby Lane with every pause.
Crab apples pulped on a cider bed,
leaves loamed with our steps, past
broken hawthorn's worm-eaten limbs
that would puff to cork if brushed
by sheep or malignant wind.
He sidled up to long-tailed tits
daring his innocence against theirs –
I hung back – smiled back at me
not knowing what to do so close.
And bramblings berrying in seasonal hues
chased on before, rampant with chaffinch,
to where we dug among the moss and docks
hoiked at nettle roots frayed as rope,
sank our saplings into Tarraby soil,
stopped the rabbits making a meal,
left them to fend quivering in
the gathering water, closing dusk.

THE FLOOD

It was a body of sorts
that bobbed in the park's waters
snagged by the fence
from its journey to the sea,
garlanded with broken trees,
a wash from the hills
of nature's recklings and prodigals
in this day's carnival of weathers.
Bucolic madness,
the kicking over of
'nature methodised',
oaks and beeches mere sprigs
on waters drunk with subversion.

As disorder evaporated,
as trees and river banks collected
themselves, we saw it was a cow
slumped at our garden's end,
its neck broken, its belly
a balloon ready to burst.

*

All highways stopped.
Water filled underpasses,
archives, erased records
of good and evil, sent
agents of the Law
to higher ground.
The lofty burgess sank
on his pillar, his Roman garb
washed with fell and gutter.

*

Nobody told them it might happen
the confluence of ceaseless storms
on the fells, the run-off from pasture
and roof, from sewers
gushing up to meet the river turning
back on itself, repulsed by the sea,
thrashing at its own tail, at its constriction.
Short circuit then, sky and street
emptied of light
as the waters brought silt creeping down
indiscernible slopes
under doors, seeping in through
air-bricks, rising through floorboards,
licking, licking, licking
memories of families, what was to come.

*

In the West the wind howls accompaniment
plays on roofs like a mouth harp
lashes the gaunt church at Moresby
high on the coast where Romans
and Lowca miners made the most
of their rotten lot, graves to the sea.
Rain gutters down valleys on waste heaps
from wasted steelworks,
too poisoned still for scrub.

*

Willows lie weeping now
along the sulking river
as chain-saws ratchet the air.
Skips fill with homes,
communities are turned to carrion
for looters and contractors.
Houses are marked with
a chemical cross, barred to families

as though infected by
the sterility of a border town when
you have to leave upon the hour.

There's a tide-mark up the hill.
I saw a salmon there, fat and silly,
ignored by crow and rat,
some sort of normality for the while perhaps.

MANNA*

The yard at seven, shifting feet like journeymen.
He'd set us to our jobs – ploughing for the lone men,
the stars with best tractors; Charles and Les, twins,
for hedging, looking after beast
(weekends they were bouncers at the Mecca,
cruel bastards); then us, the mucking gang.
We'd settled for our status, grew pride
in lowliness, always the worst van, tractors,
travelling though in lofty convoy holding traffic up
to make a point on loftier wolds
whose cattle were well-behaved,
not wild marsh creatures drunk on fogs.
Diesel would seep through cracks in hands,
cuts from baler band and spreader blades,
made them hard as tyres. Dinner on bales in sheds
at best where rats deferred, knew their place.
We liked the big estates, spread manna
on methodised vistas, saw family chapels
and Capability's bridges, racehorse dung.
We could reckon muck hill's distribution over
fields with a painter's eye, know the gear to ride,
the fall of the land. We could get the wheelings right
roll back the baize, make strips
beyond the ha-ha and industrial barn,
refashion history with our tableau.

---

* Manna is a Lincolnshire variation of 'manure'

MOLE IN THE KITCHEN

I'd seen you often enough hung
like lost gloves from barbed fence
near the disconsolate church
where rooks were hymn books
over the Sunday afternoon.

Had gathered your compost
soft and fine for pots and seeds
tripped on your mounds
full tilt in meadow race
listened at the ground to your silence.

Then the rocking chair rocked
with cats watching your paddle
round skirting boards,
your snout a bumper, toes ferocious,
skin like moleskin to cats' briar teeth.

I dropped you soft in the field
wanted to burrow for you,
give you back your dark,
watch you snuffle through
your runs beneath our knowing.

PARIAH

'A smell of sick!' they said among themselves.
Early morning bus, just me besides,
I had to agree, looked more earnestly
than them beneath the seats. 'You'd think they would
at least do the decent thing for working folk
starting out the day.'
                      I left them at the farm,
their post bags stuffed with banter and grievance.
'This job's bad enough,' I said
as we set out in the van, 'without us knowing
we're so apart. Pig muck's the worst.
They tell us more by that than any other –
cow, sheep, chicken or calf.'
That night I had to stand outside, strip off before
mother would let me in for bath and tea,
left that pariah self a heap beside
the bin until next morning's journey into scorn.

TOM

A pinch of snuff, a snort, his handkerchief
with buttons on, then Tom explodes while those
around pull back apprehensive
for pint and person. Stance resumed against

the bar, he tells another Irish joke,
looks laughing for a mirrored laugh, draws breath
and lifts his mild again. A shrug, a glance
at the clock and then his push against the crowd.

He wheels his barrow home, unloads his tools,
complaining at his dogs who whine half-blind.
No horses these, no Limber Hill which once
knew where to stop for him – *King's Head* or *Nag's*

– as well as leap the Gold Cup fences.
Tom works the gardens now for widows who
don't recognise the same weeds pushing through
day after day – the jobbing gardener's craft.

The broken pane, the gutter hanging off,
paint cracked on door and sill, mice
in the oven become at first an inconvenience
and then not even things that must get done.

* * * *

I noticed that morning his outside tap –
his only one – without a splash beneath.
We found him, long-johns down, toppled from
the bucket, his talk of Egypt and us his pals

who helped him make his stove of sand and petrol
beneath a febrile sun. We watched and listened
as the here and now silted up, the clarity,
the chill of distant desert nights close round.

CORK & STRING

We have heard across the marsh
there's been a death.
We offer our services. We do
those things you'd rather not:
block apertures, seal ducts
with cork and string.
You may think we're indecent
in our haste but we know
you can't be too soon
to prevent indiscretions.
We face the facts, have seen
how compositions
unravel on a gurgle.
We will be swift up the stairs,
we'll find the way,
we always do;
good craftsmen sniff
where they're needed,
where there's a disjunction.
Do not be ashamed
to let us in. Prurience
is not our business.
Your neighbours will learn
nothing from us
– but then they'll want
discretion for themselves.
Admit the time has come
to put away untidiness.
Life's impediments –
joy and grief – weigh us down
prevent us from getting things
in order. Look behind us
at winter's fields, shorn of crops,
fallow, hedges razored,
wheelings guttered with rain.
We like it so: so should you.

EDGAR GOES BAIT DIGGING

*'The art of our necessities is strange,
And can make vile things precious.'* – King Lear

Tines turn worm casts
in the estuary sand, mudded.
Fingers in half-light grasp

for soft, fat lugs,
broad belted for
coupling head to tail –

slimy exchange of egg,
sperm, across clitella.
Edgar slings another into

the heaving bucket, watches
muddled writhings from his haunches,
considers it necessity

to skewer them
with hooks, the barb
running up their gut.

Lines to be set before
tide's stealthy onrush
up creaks, the riches

of codling, precious inheritance,
in dark anonymous currents:
that's something yet.

III

Breccia

MAIDEN MOOR

My print on others' prints
scuff on lichen, spit on rock,
a route between tussocks
great lumps of things
demanding my attention or
over I'll go. Off to the outcrop
rare thing up here
where you ratch for a summit.
Fix position at the edge, at sweep down through
glistening bilberry, bracken mouldering,
look across the valley to crags
where climbers pin themselves,
taut on tenterhooks.
                    Quiet.
Nothing in the cup of my ear.
No wind, no sheep.
Creak of neckbones.
I turn to the moor, move on.
Plateau narrows where
ravens flap and bounce
and High Spy's pillar spies high
above Maiden Moor, a drudge
on all fours, a trudge towards
obvious summits of farther hills.

DALE HEAD

Here the peregrine haunts
above slides of slate,
abandoned decks of quarriers' huts.
Ghylls gather the seep of plateau's rain,
make pretty this incessant weeping.
The summit is a bulkhead
at the end of valleys, definer,
delimiter of communities, where tribes
have recognised a destination,
know the need to dig
into the hill's ore,
to kindle, smelt, fashion.
This is where they have arrived,
what they shall be, take names
from craft, place or,
smoothing to a hybrid tongue,
adapt their own. Fields grow
in Newlands, Buttermere, Borrowdale
like identities. Chapels emerge
in crannies of Dale Head's spurs
to look after souls calloused
by necessity's pick.
Walls delineate lower hillsides
describe with diligence contours,
boundaries reaching to
improbable heights beyond dispute.
Fell runners dash amid slimy stones
make for the breach against tarn
before crazy descent past
mine shafts, a path of their making,
a slick through bracken.

BLENCATHRA

They crossed road and track
from Threlkeld to mine village
to lob railway bolts at other boys
they saw as good for nothing else.
Enmities grew, died back,
seasonal as bracken.
Yelping like young hounds
through the clag of Blencathra
they scented trails that led
to the mine's gape
where necessity beckoned.
Hands gave up their ammunition
instead clenched chisel, hammer.
Days now measured in square setts,
lives in growing walls
from gathered stone, trimmed,
placed, fastidious, precise
until enclosures curled back
from places where walls won't go.
Like homes left in time of war
Blencathra has its scatter
of broken normality, grand hopes
left to lichen and wash of cloud.
Waste heaps pock ghylls,
a mountain mothed along its skirts.
Yet still Blencathra
rises in its saddle to mark
your arrival from the east
where broken Pennines falter,
shakes off these irritations
in a greater drama
that bubbled from the earth's core.

COLEDALE

More in these lower hills I know
bilberry fresh sprung from rampant fire
heather shoots cropped by sheep
each boggy trench, difficult step.

I know where I'll find the skull
vertebrae on the track
guess where new fallen sheep
will bloat with cairn of carrion flies.

Each rise and fall of knoll
I know as well as my own breath
that soars with the raven
yattering from the crags.

Across the valley mines cough spoil
huge dumpers skirt the scree
playthings against high Grisedale's bulk.
This I can see, being far off.

BLACK COMBE

Between Black Combe and Irish Sea
Haverigg's prison lies like flotsam,
a crate of shaken lives
from terrible storms.
We enter by the visitors' lodge
a chamber for changes from state to state.
My head still reels
at this close constriction.
Paths across the yard
define the required route
the orderliness of breathing.
Slow steps are time passing.
Here the blackened site
where once a prisoners' fire
lightened hearts,
died back into ash.
Wind passes through off the sea
by the pig farm where prisoners
learn the skill of tutelage.
Through the fence I look
towards Black Combe's slopes,
cartographed by razor wire,
imagine myself, my madness
in confinement where every glimpse
of change in heather and bracken,
every sweep of cloud that shuts off
the sun, then reveals it,
would make a sentence of a day.
What relief the driving rain would be
that hangs like sheets over the fence line.
That would stop my longing
to range between summits
to mine my strength up the track,
and look toward Duddon, Ennerdale,
then lunge down between ghylls

giddy with movement.
At any rate I can leave now,
shake off the prison's chill as
doors thud shut, climb up
Black Combe, look back down
to the prison, miniature on fields
between mountain and serrated sea.

SKIDDAW

Absently I skim a slate,
lichened, wet, keen across bilberry
back up scree into cloud.
How can I understand
the way great sheets of sediment
compounded, compacted,
tilted, folded, were flung out
of axis by earth's trauma
into inclinations where
all's possible? Rocks break,
fold, pucker. Faults are exploited
and lava leeches in.
Slow the cooling for birth
of crystal, granite.
Skiddaw's slates lie round me
distracted, compass needles
without their lodestar,
disoriented fragments
of endless reconstruction.
How slowly the sea bed moves,
debris held back for
earth to rend earth's crust again.
Again burst lava, dust, volcanic ash,
and still re-form
– breccia, tuff, rhyolites.
Can we understand in our flicker of time
the build up from the North,
Caledonian pressure that made
softer beds fold, whilst those
of sterner stuff arched up?

And this is where we are,
what we call Skiddaw,

the axis around which
seas formed, landlocked with their catches,
where ranges of hills thrust high.
Even then Devonian deserts
obliterate what had seemed
an architecture of sorts.
Glaciers came, excoriating valleys,
shifting granite, slate, erratics
until the retreat from
Skiddaw's peak. Rain softened
slopes and lakes, made it easier
to be vain in our understanding.

CAUSEY PIKE

Before early haze filters the brilliance of things –
scree and each feeling ghyll in hills I know –
I slow my running before Causey's fist. A day
such as this, sun livening skin, shoulders,
sway of hips, skip over shards of time.

HELVELLYN

The power of hills is on thee. Wordsworth: To -------- On Her First Ascent to the Summit of Helvellyn

Too early for the hordes
I walk about the plateau
look down on Helvellyn's watch-towers
mist swirling clear
of Swirral and Striding Edge.
Red Tarn, gathered by ridges
lies still, in a bath of sun.
Adventurers' voices reach me
echoing against the cove
where Gough's dog once sat
watching the flesh drop
from his master's corpse.
Scott, Wordsworth wrote of it.
I read the words on memorial slab,
themselves softening in all weathers.
I think too of the brothers parting,
William and John, below
at Grisedale, feel trapped
in others' elegies. I turn away.
I had come here by a different route,
picked my time and felt the slow
revelation of lower slopes
as morning grew, and scarred tracks
gave way to choice across the fells.
There are many ways to a summit;
even then there's more joy
in choice and wrong choosing
than in triumphal arrival.

KIDSTY PIKE

Its own weathers urgent still
as lower ground falls vapid
in the staleness of summer.
Cloud sweeps rain fine
as sweat from loftier crags
across bilberry and gruff
where sheep crop round
a bloated other. Hefted here
they watch our passing
like a turn of sky, just as
they watched men pass
to High Street races
or a flock of Romans
gather their highest road.
Bog cotton flares our path
to the pike's cusp, we seeing
nothing here but breath,
stones, plants as wilful,
and the thronged skies.

CARROCK FELL

Here the mountains sighed their last,
sending boulders, errant baggage,
to Mosedale's plain,
defiant bullies in the pasture.
Up Rake's Trod I slip past
the scree, quiet in case it wakes
— held in imminence —
then under the lofty pine,
a standard on the ramparts
of this minor castle,
an outpost of imperial hills.

The ghyll chatters on its way
to the Caldew's tribal gathering.
Slime on the rocks which
only glimpse the sun on the brightest day.
Lichens cluster like old tales
on upstart birch, bracken waylays
innocent steps.

I recite the names — wolfram,
gabbro, feldspar, gramophyre —
sounds that shimmer with stories
folded into this broken fell, *carraig*,
a taste of the ghyll and the mist
lapping my throat.

On the top a guesswork of stones
gathered to a fort by tribes
who faced others from the east
eager to know where the wind came from,
relentless as glaciers,
certain of the need to climb.

CALDBECK FELLS

This moment now, skylark singing,
wheatears' chat and dip on rocks
in fading gorse.
A scree of crows making hay
of moss on softer hills,
yellow cinquefoils precious
in reeds bent to the wind.
Nubs of rock glisten white
through grass, ask for definition
which I ignore. A time for pleasure,
abandonment on such a day.
Enough of a late spring
with the threat of rain passing Skiddaw
from the coast, high above
High Pike over Carrock Fell's
ancient castle site where
hang gliders sally.
Glenderaterra, Glenderamackin,
Caldew run like veins
of galina in valley bottoms,
Sharp Edge a jagged tooth
in Blencathra's jaw.
Knott's mounded bulk hides
the pass of Trusmador
where blighted lovers
must have played their roles.
Along mining tracks I see my sons
cycling, running, making continuities
landscapes of their own.

IV

COURBET IN SAINTE-PÉLAGIE PRISON

I have never seen an angel
but I see this bowl,
these apples and pomegranate.

I have time enough.
My sisters bring me food.
I have solitude.

I can arrange this fruit
as I wish, leave
the pomegranate

outside the bowl or in,
watch the skin colour change
with the hours, with

what light there is.
And should I miss
the best of the morning

on the tankard, no matter;
tomorrow I'll fix
how it will be then, not now.

I am after all painting
what I know for though
we have dreams, fancies

they can lie like ruined
pillars, monuments
to vanities,

best friends sag dead
against cemetery walls
and the state turn viper.

So though I paint
this still-life, I fix
the time when I knew all this

when my apples and pomegranate
breathed in my room
and the light changed for us all.

A BURIAL AT ORNANS

after the painting by Courbet

Come, sisters, you shall be there
weeping with fresh handkerchiefs,
a vase of tenderness in front of
those old gnarled bonnets. I'll have the dog
tie you in with a doleful gaze
as it stands besides my republican friends.
You, the mayor, shall be in the centre
as you would wish, Claude-Hélène-Prosper,
as you told me when you came
to my door. But I shall set you back.
You will compete with the beadles' noses,
red as their robes, their fluted hats,
looking this way and that.
I'll not forget Christ high above
the sacristan, hoist on his cross and staked
on the horizon, another crucifixion.
Nor the bearers with their winding sheets,
boys enquiring into their shielded eyes.
I'll have the coffin brought in
from the left where my dead Oudot
will look on, dear grandfather.
Parents too, I'll bring you in to wait
for the abbé's words, coffin's approach.

But, Antoine-Joseph, it's you who will squat
beside the gaping grave, pulled away
from your vines for the extra cash,
you who wait to sink another friend.
You will be set by your trap,
hand on knee, gaze fixed
on open prayer book, its spring of words.
And the skull, dug out from this new graveyard,
shall wait for a fellow.

I'll lose some friends by this:
those who see a clique, those who think
I bury principles, those who only see
my ugliness. *Tant pis!* for they should know,
as should you, the grave will have no end;
frame as you will, it will reach
out as open as the sky beyond.

THE STONE-BREAKERS

1

It was to have been a landscape
that day, a ride out
from Ornans to frame a moment.

But they were by the road,
one young, one old. I could go
no further, such misery, destitution.

A morning here was all their life:
how they began, how they would end.
His meagre hammer raised, he cleft

the stones that lay about.
Some order in this I supposed
but I conjectured how long

he might go on until the boy
should lay down his basket
pick up the hammer for himself.

It was my delight when they agreed
to pose next day. I only
wanted them in working clothes:

straw hat, cracked sabots
blue socks with holes at the heel,
patched trousers, torn shirt,

the boy with his one brace across.
Then round about, their pan,
adze, broken shovel, basket

and loaf of bread with spoon
the colour of the rocks.
But I did not show their faces:

they spoke for more than
themselves, roused pity from injustice,
stayed half-turned, in shade.

2 Gagey

It was just another day when
he came by, the painter, M. Courbet.
What he saw in us I cannot tell.

We went along next day
in our usual things, with tools
baskets, and struck our pose.

Bloody hard it was to keep still,
hammer raised above the stones
he'd arranged beside some bread.

At least he knew to make a cushion
of some straw for my knee.
Those trousers have had it

near enough, patches on patches.
But he wouldn't let us change,
wouldn't let us show our faces.

3

Old Gagey was game, so
I thought, why not?
Gets us out of the sun

away from the dust, the damn
chink of hammer, the splinters
of stone in your eye.

Nice bloke, lots of good dinners
in him, didn't patronise.
Odd, though, us having to pose

just as we do each day.
Who would want to know?
We're nothing, are we?

Just two stone-breakers
stuck on a road, turning
a landscape into pebbles.

THE CATALOGUE

For Nick Volley

View from the studio

Slant on to window, past the downpipe
and London bricks burnt to Mediterranean browns
it's the broken pane in the street beyond
that catches the eye.

Self portrait and cast

A clutch of brushes and knives,
apple and glass on studio stool
before truncated nude,
you behind in the mirror.

Self portrait with cast and jug

To the side this time, it's your blurred face
and shoes in the reflected black of the studio
that attract us. The cast fades into the foreground.

Pheasants

Cock and hen – necks hanging over
marble top, with pan, knife
and garlic – await their dressing.

Still life with black jug

The whitewashed wall will take anything
against it: colander, basket, broken bread,
knife and onion, and the studio pan ready.

Still life, curtain and chair

Heavy drape, oil lamp,
roses in a glass, flat basket
with fruit, tablecloth turned up.
Who will sit in the chair?

*   *   *

And then it's work in progress –
Sylvia sleeping a sleep of troubles
beside the window to the garden
where the washing line bisects the tree
lawn pinioned by the sundial.

                You stand back, wait
to see who I am now by what I say.

Talk of years since last we met,
lives not arranged as we might want
though we pretend to composition, a palette by design.
Instead the light is incidental
textures applied too thick
props not of our choosing,
perspective askew
and we, the subjects, looking on.

PICTURES AT AN EXHIBITION

Abbot Hall Gallery, Kendal, 21st April 2005

The casement window leads the eye to
the sculpted chimney, a *trompe l'oeil*
since closed to smoke.
Slabs of lead bend
to softer parts of the roof
where textures are porous,
thickly applied, where slate has given way
to softer hues. Beyond
the magnolia loses another petal
to those arranged
across the tarmac path,
careful lawns. The gaze
is taken to the cyclist in
middle distance crossing
a latticed bridge above
the brilliant Kent. A mother stops
at an angle to the river,
tucks the blanket round her child,
moves on. The broken castle
adds to the picturesque
before the steeper slopes of Benson Knott
where town yields to fell.
Warm smells of oils are redolent
of paintings, draw us back
to matters in hand.

DRAWINGS AT AN EXHIBITION

Abbot Hall Gallery, Kendal 25th April 2006

i.m. Nicholas Volley

None of yours here among
the charcoals, pastels, etchings,
the beards of Sikhs intricate
as temples, the table lamps, misericordia,
a map of England drawn from memory.
A celebration this of the line,
clarity of purpose that eschews
all vanity. And so
in a way I think of you
in that Spitalfields studio,
oils, pans, fruit bowls
that might be out of Courbet,
and the canvasses that wait for you to speak.
The palette hardens now.
Daft sod! how dare you go
when your sort's just what we need
among the clamour of the fleeting day,
the image that flickers and is gone?
Some comfort here, I suppose,
in seeing others who can measure distance,
worth, put in perspective, and know
that in the shift of pencil, charcoal or engraving tool
they make a mark, speak.

FISH

1

Strange, they say, the feeling
first time you sink the knife
into the quivering belly,
slice upwards to gawping gills,
pull out guts, warm, still working,
then over the edge for gulls.
Some give an anaesthetic blow,
conscience's quibble.

2

As though out of Chardin
the cat is arched over sink and stove
insistent about the pan
of tongues and cheeks, gluey
in steam. On the slab
they were pearls of flesh
against the fillets' vulgarity.
Only purses of roe
could rival their discretion.

3

The kipper is by Picasso
each surface displayed
on a comb of bone,
fins relocated
to extremes, head
separated. Turn
it over though
and those eyes watch
from here, and there.